Success Journal

from Inspiration House

Anjani Ali

AuthorHouse™
1663 Liberty Drive
Bloomington, IN 47403
www.authorhouse.com
Phone: 1-800-839-8640

Published by AuthorHouse 12/26/2013

ISBN: 978-1-4918-3696-5 (sc)
ISBN: 978-1-4918-3697-2 (e)

Library of Congress Control Number: 2013920741

authorHOUSE®

All things are Possible........

Your Future is Determined by your daily activity!

Goal Setting

Goal setting sets the paste to make your dreams become a reality. The mind conceives the idea but a plan must be implemented. As the old saying goes a pilot cannot just take an aircraft and fly anywhere. There must be a flight plan and it must be clear.

Decide what you love to do, take the chance to pursue it, you have nothing to loose.

Think back for a moment at the times in your life when you fantasized about something and now you are actually living that fantasy, it has become a reality.

Focus and Activity is your only means of attracting the right people and finding yourself in the right place at the right time. If you don't get up and start walking you won't get to the other end of the room.

Creating a plan sends a message to that part of your mind that might doubt the possibility that you can make your dreams a reality.

See your truth for your life whatever it is in your imagination and believe that all things are possible, feel the emotion of it and speak and think as if it was real.

Create Affirmations

Create a plan

Work the plan

Look the part

Dress the part

Act the part

Be truthful about it

Talk to God about it openly and sincerely

and magically you will start seeing opportunities coming your way.

Writing down these goals serves as a constant reminder of what you want out of your life!

You have one life and a certain amount of time, what are you going to do with it.

This journal seeks to guide you.

Best Wishes!!

(Matthew 7:7 - "Ask and it will be given to you; seek and you will find, knock and it will be opened to you:)

I had a dream that my life could be better and happier. I searched for six years for a way and one day it all became a reality. You are holding that reality in your hands right now. Keep seeking, it's worth it!

Encouragement for the Journey

- All things are possible.

- Forgiveness is freedom, forgive and let it go, it is for your own good.

- Meditate constantly on the positive things around you.

- Judge not, you don't know what you would do if you were in that situation.

- Exercise Self Control.

- Religion is a discipline, take time to go through the processes in life.

- Success is a discipline. Practice doing things right.

- Death and life lies in the power of the tongue, watch what you say.

- Pray for clarity, insight, wisdom, confidence and resources to create the life you want.

- Always wear an attitude of gratitude no matter how unfavorable things may seem.

- If you don't practice the lessons life has taught you then you haven't learnt anything.

- This is the day the lord has made, live it

- Jesus said that he came that we might ALL have life and have it in abundance, to the full until it overflows.   - Something worth holding on to.

- I can do all things through he who strengthen me.

- If he can do it for another he can do it for you.

- Your personal relationship with God is important, be truthful to him, tell him how you really feel. Tell him what hurts.

- Love yourself – treat yourself.

- Find ways to uplift yourself all the time.

- Dress up or go to a nice restaurant when you are feeling down.

- Be the one to make peace first. Be the one to display affection first in your everyday life.

List of Desired Life Accomplishments

Home

Vacation Home

Pay Cheque

Vehicles

Family (healthy, happy, safe, successful)

Kids (healthy, happy, safe, successful)

Money (Savings, investments, bank balances)

Promotion

Education (Degree, Masters, Ph.D)

Weight

Health

Relationships (Spouse, siblings, children, parents)

Spirituality

(character traits to develop, life lesson to practice, etc.)

Accomplishments to Date

Home _____

Vacation Home _____

Pay Cheque _____

Vehicles _____

Family (healthy, happy, safe, successful) _____

Kids (healthy, happy, safe, successful) _____

Money

(Savings, investments, bank balances) _____

_____

Promotion _____

Education (Degree, Masters, Ph.D) _____

Weight _____

Health _____

Relationships

(Spouse, siblings, children, parents) _____

Spirituality (character traits to develop,

life lesson to practice, etc.) _____

What can I do better now To get closer to achieving my goals

Home _____

_____

_____

Vacation Home _____

_____

_____

Pay Cheque _____

_____

_____

Motor Vehicles _____

_____

_____

Family _____

_____

_____

Kids _____

_____

_____

Money _____

_____

_____

Promotion _____

_____

_____

Education _____

_____

Weight

        _____

Health

        _____

Relationships

        _____

Spirituality

        _____

Other

        _____

Other

        _____

Other

        _____

Words of Affirmation

Based on your desired goals, write down the positive things you will say to yourself for encouragement, for example: "I will get my degree in Management by June 2013." "I will lose 10 pounds in six (6) months. Or "I would have read three (3) inspirational books within the next three (3) weeks."

Affirm your character traits: (Say: "I am strong, intelligent, focused, etc.)

Start Affirming:

_____

_____

_____

_____

_____

_____

_____

_____

_____

_____

_____

_____

_____

Monthly Budget

Item	Monthly	Quarterly	Semi-Annually	Annually	Totals
Mortgage 1					
Mortgage 2					
Life Insurance 1					
Life Insurance 2					
Life Insurance 3					
Major Medical					
Annuity 1					
Annuity 2					
Other					
Groceries					
Fruits					
Fuel/Gas/Travel					
Electricity					
Water					
Other					
Personal Allowance					
Charity					
Clothing					
Eating Out					
Entertainment					
Stationery/Books/ Tapes, etc.					
Gifts: Birthdays/Charity					
Vacation					
Savings					
CHILDREN:					
Snacks					
School Fees					
Baby Sitter					
Medication/Vitamins					
Baby Food/milk					
Diapers					
Recreation					
School Functions/donations					
Birthday parties					
TOTALS					

BUDGET TRACKING

	Jan.	Feb.	March	April	May	June	July	Aug.	Sept.	Oct.	Nov.	Dec.
Mortgage 1												
Mortgage 2												
Life Insurance 1												
Life Insurance 2												
Life Insurance 3												
Major Medical												
Annuity 1												
Annuity 2												
Other												
Groceries												
Fruits												
Fuel/Gas/												
Travel												
Electricity												
Water												
Other												
Personal Allowance												
Charity												
Clothing												
Eating Out												
Entertainment												
Stationery/ Books/												
Tapes, etc.												
Gifts: Birthdays												

Charity												
Vacation												
Savings												
CHILDREN												
Snacks												
School Fees												
Baby Sitter												
Medication/ Vitamins												
Baby Food/milk												
Diapers												
Recreation												
School Functions/ Donations												
Birthday parties												
TOTALS												

(Place a tick or the amount in the boxes of the bills you paid for the respective months. This will help you know what is outstanding or paid already)

Notes: _____

_____

_____

_____

_____

Short Term Action Plan to Achieve Goals

_____
_____
_____
_____
_____
_____
_____
_____
_____
_____
_____
_____
_____
_____
_____
_____
_____
_____
_____
_____
_____

Medium Term Action Plan to Achieve Goals

Long Term Action Plan to Achieve Goals

_____
_____
_____
_____
_____
_____
_____
_____
_____
_____
_____
_____
_____
_____
_____
_____
_____
_____
_____
_____
_____
_____
_____
_____

Daily Activity Record

*** Do Something everyday to take you closer to your goals***

JANUARY

WEEK 1							
	Sunday						
	Monday						
	Tuesday						
	Wednesday						
	Thursday						
	Friday						
	Saturday						
WEEK 2							
	Sunday						
	Monday						
	Tuesday						
	Wednesday						
	Thursday						
	Friday						
	Saturday						
WEEK 3							
	Sunday						
	Monday						
	Tuesday						
	Wednesday						
	Thursday						
	Friday						
	Saturday						
WEEK 4							
	Sunday						
	Monday						
	Tuesday						
	Wednesday						
	Thursday						
	Friday						
	Saturday						
WEEK 5							
	Sunday						
	Monday						
	Tuesday						
	Wednesday						
	Thursday						
	Friday						
	Saturday						

Despise not the day of small beginnings....

FEBRUARY

WEEK 1							
	Sunday						
	Monday						
	Tuesday						
	Wednesday						
	Thursday						
	Friday						
	Saturday						
WEEK 2							
	Sunday						
	Monday						
	Tuesday						
	Wednesday						
	Thursday						
	Friday						
	Saturday						
WEEK 3							
	Sunday						
	Monday						
	Tuesday						
	Wednesday						
	Thursday						
	Friday						
	Saturday						
WEEK 4							
	Sunday						
	Monday						
	Tuesday						
	Wednesday						
	Thursday						
	Friday						
	Saturday						
WEEK 5							
	Sunday						
	Monday						
	Tuesday						
	Wednesday						
	Thursday						
	Friday						
	Saturday						

Let no one speak Negativity to you, your environment or your dreams....

MARCH

WEEK 1						
	Sunday					
	Monday					
	Tuesday					
	Wednesday					
	Thursday					
	Friday					
	Saturday					
WEEK 2						
	Sunday					
	Monday					
	Tuesday					
	Wednesday					
	Thursday					
	Friday					
	Saturday					
WEEK 3						
	Sunday					
	Monday					
	Tuesday					
	Wednesday					
	Thursday					
	Friday					
	Saturday					
WEEK 4						
	Sunday					
	Monday					
	Tuesday					
	Wednesday					
	Thursday					
	Friday					
	Saturday					
WEEK 5						
	Sunday					
	Monday					
	Tuesday					
	Wednesday					
	Thursday					
	Friday					
	Saturday					

If you do nothing you get nothing...

*** Do Something everyday to take you closer to your goals***

APRIL

WEEK 1							
	Sunday						
	Monday						
	Tuesday						
	Wednesday						
	Thursday						
	Friday						
	Saturday						
WEEK 2							
	Sunday						
	Monday						
	Tuesday						
	Wednesday						
	Thursday						
	Friday						
	Saturday						
WEEK 3							
	Sunday						
	Monday						
	Tuesday						
	Wednesday						
	Thursday						
	Friday						
	Saturday						
WEEK 4							
	Sunday						
	Monday						
	Tuesday						
	Wednesday						
	Thursday						
	Friday						
	Saturday						
WEEK 5							
	Sunday						
	Monday						
	Tuesday						
	Wednesday						
	Thursday						
	Friday						
	Saturday						

I pledge to take life and my goals one day at a time until I accomplish them...

Do Something everyday to take you closer to your goals

MAY

WEEK 1						
	Sunday					
	Monday					
	Tuesday					
	Wednesday					
	Thursday					
	Friday					
	Saturday					
WEEK 2						
	Sunday					
	Monday					
	Tuesday					
	Wednesday					
	Thursday					
	Friday					
	Saturday					
WEEK 3						
	Sunday					
	Monday					
	Tuesday					
	Wednesday					
	Thursday					
	Friday					
	Saturday					
WEEK 4						
	Sunday					
	Monday					
	Tuesday					
	Wednesday					
	Thursday					
	Friday					
	Saturday					
WEEK 5						
	Sunday					
	Monday					
	Tuesday					
	Wednesday					
	Thursday					
	Friday					
	Saturday					

This is the life my God has given me I will honor it...

JUNE

WEEK 1							
	Sunday						
	Monday						
	Tuesday						
	Wednesday						
	Thursday						
	Friday						
	Saturday						
WEEK 2							
	Sunday						
	Monday						
	Tuesday						
	Wednesday						
	Thursday						
	Friday						
	Saturday						
WEEK 3							
	Sunday						
	Monday						
	Tuesday						
	Wednesday						
	Thursday						
	Friday						
	Saturday						
WEEK 4							
	Sunday						
	Monday						
	Tuesday						
	Wednesday						
	Thursday						
	Friday						
	Saturday						
WEEK 5							
	Sunday						
	Monday						
	Tuesday						
	Wednesday						
	Thursday						
	Friday						
	Saturday						

My Majic Seed is this life and now, my tomorrow is what I make of it....

JULY

WEEK 1							
	Sunday						
	Monday						
	Tuesday						
	Wednesday						
	Thursday						
	Friday						
	Saturday						
WEEK 2							
	Sunday						
	Monday						
	Tuesday						
	Wednesday						
	Thursday						
	Friday						
	Saturday						
WEEK 3							
	Sunday						
	Monday						
	Tuesday						
	Wednesday						
	Thursday						
	Friday						
	Saturday						
WEEK 4							
	Sunday						
	Monday						
	Tuesday						
	Wednesday						
	Thursday						
	Friday						
	Saturday						
WEEK 5							
	Sunday						
	Monday						
	Tuesday						
	Wednesday						
	Thursday						
	Friday						
	Saturday						

If I want to get to the other side of the room I have to start walking toward the other side.....

** *Do Something everyday to take you closer to your goals**

AUGUST

WEEK 1							
	Sunday						
	Monday						
	Tuesday						
	Wednesday						
	Thursday						
	Friday						
	Saturday						
WEEK 2							
	Sunday						
	Monday						
	Tuesday						
	Wednesday						
	Thursday						
	Friday						
	Saturday						
WEEK 3							
	Sunday						
	Monday						
	Tuesday						
	Wednesday						
	Thursday						
	Friday						
	Saturday						
WEEK 4							
	Sunday						
	Monday						
	Tuesday						
	Wednesday						
	Thursday						
	Friday						
	Saturday						
WEEK 5							
	Sunday						
	Monday						
	Tuesday						
	Wednesday						
	Thursday						
	Friday						
	Saturday						

I shall renew my mind this day with positive thoughts....

*** Do Something everyday to take you closer to your goals***

SEPTEMBER

WEEK 1						
	Sunday					
	Monday					
	Tuesday					
	Wednesday					
	Thursday					
	Friday					
	Saturday					
WEEK 2						
	Sunday					
	Monday					
	Tuesday					
	Wednesday					
	Thursday					
	Friday					
	Saturday					
WEEK 3						
	Sunday					
	Monday					
	Tuesday					
	Wednesday					
	Thursday					
	Friday					
	Saturday					
WEEK 4						
	Sunday					
	Monday					
	Tuesday					
	Wednesday					
	Thursday					
	Friday					
	Saturday					
WEEK 5						
	Sunday					
	Monday					
	Tuesday					
	Wednesday					
	Thursday					
	Friday					
	Saturday					

No Action, No Change....

OCTOBER

WEEK 1							
	Sunday						
	Monday						
	Tuesday						
	Wednesday						
	Thursday						
	Friday						
	Saturday						
WEEK 2							
	Sunday						
	Monday						
	Tuesday						
	Wednesday						
	Thursday						
	Friday						
	Saturday						
WEEK 3							
	Sunday						
	Monday						
	Tuesday						
	Wednesday						
	Thursday						
	Friday						
	Saturday						
WEEK 4							
	Sunday						
	Monday						
	Tuesday						
	Wednesday						
	Thursday						
	Friday						
	Saturday						
WEEK 5							
	Sunday						
	Monday						
	Tuesday						
	Wednesday						
	Thursday						
	Friday						
	Saturday						

Despair is not of God, cast it out...

Do Something everyday to take you closer to your goals

NOVEMBER

WEEK 1							
	Sunday						
	Monday						
	Tuesday						
	Wednesday						
	Thursday						
	Friday						
	Saturday						
WEEK 2							
	Sunday						
	Monday						
	Tuesday						
	Wednesday						
	Thursday						
	Friday						
	Saturday						
WEEK 3							
	Sunday						
	Monday						
	Tuesday						
	Wednesday						
	Thursday						
	Friday						
	Saturday						
WEEK 4							
	Sunday						
	Monday						
	Tuesday						
	Wednesday						
	Thursday						
	Friday						
	Saturday						
WEEK 5							
	Sunday						
	Monday						
	Tuesday						
	Wednesday						
	Thursday						
	Friday						
	Saturday						

Hard work always pay off...

DECEMBER

WEEK 1							
	Sunday						
	Monday						
	Tuesday						
	Wednesday						
	Thursday						
	Friday						
	Saturday						
WEEK 2							
	Sunday						
	Monday						
	Tuesday						
	Wednesday						
	Thursday						
	Friday						
	Saturday						
WEEK 3							
	Sunday						
	Monday						
	Tuesday						
	Wednesday						
	Thursday						
	Friday						
	Saturday						
WEEK 4							
	Sunday						
	Monday						
	Tuesday						
	Wednesday						
	Thursday						
	Friday						
	Saturday						
WEEK 5							
	Sunday						
	Monday						
	Tuesday						
	Wednesday						
	Thursday						
	Friday						
	Saturday						

This is the day the Lord has given me, I will be grateful that I have life!

Notes

Notes

Notes

Notes

Notes

Notes

Notes

Notes

Notes

Notes

Wish Book

INSPIRATION HOUSE

Start Visualizing the Life you want for Yourself!!

Affirmations

√   *I have clarity*

√   *The Universe is working in my Favor*

√   *I am living my Purpose*

√   *I am healthy*

√   *I am Happy*

√   *My life is balanced*

√   *I have compatible and Supportive Friends, Family, Spouse and Business Associates*

√   *My children are educated, healthy and happy*

(Continue with your personal affirmations)

_____

_____

_____

_____

_____

_____

_____

_____

_____

_____

_____

_____

_____

Encouragement for the Journey

→   *Forgiveness is Freedom.*

→   *When we pay a price for something we usually get back ten fold of good.*

→   *Meditate on the positive things around you.*

→   *Don't judge others, we never know when what would happen to us.*

→   *Exercise self control.*

→   *Religion is a discipline: Discipline = Success.*

→   *Death and Life lies in the power of the tongue, choose life (speak positive, be grateful).*

→   *Ones Soul can be affected by ones words.*

→   *Give everything you do your best. Mediocrity has no place in the life of successful people.*

→   *Pray for clarity, insight, wisdom, confidence and resources to create the life you want.*

→   *Always wear an attitude of gratitude.*

→   *If you don't practice the lessons life experiences have taught you then you haven't learn't anything.*

→   *Enjoy where you are in life and do your best, there is an unseen reason for it.*

→   *Do not bow down to fear.*

→   *In times of despair, take one tiny step at a time.*

My Pay Cheque

(You can create your own cheque with name and amount you desire)

My Home

(Obtain photos of house plans and images from Internet and books, etc.)

Details of my Home

(Place pictures of the inside of your home on the following blank sheets)

√   *Colour of walls, use strips from Paint Shop*

√   *Rugs*

√   *Carpet*

√   *Tiles*

√   *Wall Paintings*

√   *Flowers*

√   *Drapes*

√   *Bedding, etc.*

Note: *These can be obtained from Internet/Catalogs/Magazines/Books.*

Place Photo here.....................

Place Photo here.....................

Place Photo here....................

Place Photo here.....................

Place Photo here.....................

Place Photo here....................

Place Photo here......................

Place Photo here.....................

Place Photo here.....................

Place Photo here.....................

My Motor Vehicle

Make: _____

Model: _____

Colour: _____

Date Purchased: _____

My Qualifications

Course 1: _____

Start Date: _____

Completion Date: _____

Course 2: _____

Start Date: _____

Completion Date: _____

Degree: _____

Start Date: _____

Completion Date: _____

Degree: _____

Start Date: _____

Completion Date: _____

Masters: _____

Start Date: _____

Completion Date: _____

Ph.D: _____

Start Date: _____

Completion Date: _____

Other: _____

Start Date: _____

Completion Date: _____

Other: _____

Start Date: _____

Completion Date: _____

Details of my Vacation Destinations

(Place pictures of Cruise Ships, Resorts, Spas, Nature hikes, etc. on the following pages – be sure to write destination dates)

Place Pictures in here

Destination: _____

Departure Date: _____

Details: _____

_____

_____

_____

_____

_____

_____

_____

_____

_____

Place Pictures in here

Destination: _____

Departure Date: _____

Details: _____

_____

_____

_____

_____

_____

_____

_____

_____

_____

Place Pictures in here

Destination: _____

Departure Date: _____

Details: _____

_____

_____

_____

_____

_____

_____

_____

_____

Place Pictures in here

Destination: _____

Departure Date: _____

Details: _____

_____

_____

_____

_____

_____

_____

_____

_____

_____

Place Pictures in here

Destination: _____

Departure Date: _____

Details: _____

_____

_____

_____

_____

_____

_____

_____

_____

Place Pictures in here

Destination: _____

Departure Date: _____

Details: _____

_____

_____

_____

_____

_____

_____

_____

_____

_____

Place Pictures in here

Destination: _____

Departure Date: _____

Details: _____

_____

_____

_____

_____

_____

_____

_____

_____

Place Pictures in here

Destination: _____

Departure Date: _____

Details: _____

_____

_____

_____

_____

_____

_____

_____

_____

_____

Place Pictures in here

Destination: _____

Departure Date: _____

Details: _____

_____

_____

_____

_____

_____

_____

_____

_____

My Bank Account Statement

Sketch how you would like your bank statement to look. (If possible photocopy an old statement, white off figures and date, then re-enter the figures you would like to see)

Write an autobiography on the next few pages,
then rewrite it to sound the way you wish.

See It!

Believe It!

Achieve It!